INSTITUTE FOR PUBLIC POLICY RESEARCH

Education:
A Different
Vision

An Alternative
White Paper

CONTENTS

Section 1

Section 2

INTRODUCTION

In the run up to the 1992 General Election, fourteen professors of education and allied disciplines from universities around the country wrote a letter to *The Guardian.*

In their letter they declared: 'a modern society cannot prosper with a narrow education base and socially divisive hierarchies of schools. High quality education is an essential investment in the skills and knowledge needed to cope with the challenges of the next century. It must not be reserved for some children in some of our schools.'

They went on to express their belief that we needed a Government 'which treats education as a public service and not as a commodity to be "traded" in the market place, which is seriously committed to high standards in that service, which rejects the creation of escape routes for the few while the main system crumbles and which refuses to subject schools to "free market" or any other dogmas.'

Like countless others with an interest or involvement in education, the signatories to that letter were disappointed to see the newly elected Conservative Government move even further in its determination to subject schools to the operation of 'market forces'.

Disregarding most of the submissions made in response to its White Paper, *Choice and Diversity*, the Government has embodied in yet another Education Act proposals which do little to address the basic needs and weaknesses of our educational system and which could do much to threaten the very existence of the system itself.

In keeping with the beliefs they expressed in their letter to *The Guardian*, the signatories reject the philosophy and most of the proposals in the Act. They insist that there is a more enlightened way of looking at education, one which would have as its aim improving the quality of education for *all* children, opening up of greater opportunities for *all* citizens, and the achievement of the higher educational standards which our rapidly changing society will demand to meet the challenges of the 21st century.

They have therefore joined together to put forward an alternative to the Government's programme, one which will bring educational advance rather than the regression to past and discredited practices favoured by the Government, and which is derived from a philosophy and set of values radically different from that set out in the White Paper.

Unlike the Government, they believe it is necessary to look at the whole of educational provision as a coherent and just system, to see education as a life-long process which should begin with pre-school education and be carried through to a wide variety of forms of continuing and adult education.

Their report is based on initial papers prepared by individual members of the group. The final text has been written and edited by Professor Ted Wragg, with the assistance of Fred Jarvis, former General Secretary of the National Union of Teachers, who has acted as Secretary of the group.

While the individual members of the group do not necessarily endorse every statement and proposal in the various sections of the report, they are all agreed on the main conclusions and recommendations.

CONTRIBUTORS

Stephen Ball	King's College, London
Tim Brighouse	Keele University
John Bynner	City University
Frank Coffield	Durham University
Tony Edwards	Newcastle University
John Elliott	East Anglia University
Harvey Goldstein	Institute of Education, London
Gerald Grace	Durham University
Fred Jarvis (secretary)	Former General Secretary, NUT
Richard Pring	Oxford University
Elizabeth Smith	Exeter University
John Tomlinson	Warwick University
Sally Tomlinson	Goldsmith's College, London
Geoff Whitty	Institute of Education, London
Ted Wragg (editor)	Exeter University

Professor A H Halsey of Nuffield College was one of the signatories of the letter to the Guardian but was prevented by ill health from contributing to the paper. However, he fully supports this report and its conclusions.

This alternative White Paper is in two sections. The first deals
with the principles on which education should be founded,
discussing such questions as:

- What is the vision of life in the 21st century?
- What are the values and philosophy that should underpin education?
- Who should hold power and how should it be used?
- How should the education service be accountable?
- What should be provided privately and publicly?
- What is the role of parents and governors?

The second section covers both the process of education and the
service, providing proposals on such key issues as:

- What form should pre-school education take?
- What should be the nature of primary and secondary schooling?
- What kind of post-compulsory further and higher education should be offered to younger and older adults?
- How should education be organised?
- What forms of examination and testing are appropriate?
- What should be done for children with special educational needs?
- How should we train and retrain teachers?

SECTION 1

PREFACE

The 1992 White Paper *Choice and Diversity* was unique among White Papers in its resemblance to a party political pamphlet. Lacking any pretence of seeking consensus apart from its appeal to 'commonsense principles', it set out a 'new framework for schools', which was shaped largely by ideological prejudice and sectarian dogma. Yet what was presented as a 'great programme of reform', beginning in 1979 and reaching its culmination with the 1993 Education Act, is based on a limited and socially divisive set of principles.

The purpose of this alternative vision is to set out the very different principles on which public education should be founded, and then to outline the very different 'framework' which would be built from them. Before doing so, we outline the 'vision' being offered by the present Government.

Its 'five great themes' are identified as quality, diversity, increased parental choice, greater autonomy for schools and greater accountability by schools. They are introduced by the Prime Minister as resting on 'commonsense'. That is, they are so obviously good and sensible that opposition to them can be dismissed as the self-interest of 'producers' whose hold over education is being so 'successfully' challenged. And as words, they may indeed seem as hard to reject as 'virtue' or 'truth'. Yet the real effects of the 1993 Education Act will be, and are intended to be, very different.

The rhetoric is that 'parents know best' what is in the interests of their children. Within the context of a National Curriculum more extensive and more obsessively tested than in any country, that rhetoric is hard to translate into reality. The Government's evident disdain for parents' opinions about the form, frequency and publicising of tests, as evidenced by John Patten's reference to the views of the national leaders of the Parent-Teacher Associations as 'Neanderthal', make the translation more difficult still. It also reflects the huge and continuing increase in state control which recent legislation is bringing about. Since 1988, the Secretary of State has acquired several hundred more powers and, ominously, sole responsibility for educational provision rather than a shared responsibility with locally-elected Authorities. Policy has been driven, as was much of the 1988 Reform Act, by a deep dislike of local government (which is considered to be too often resistant to the Government's wishes) and a marked preference for unaccountable quangos which can be well-filled with advisers whose main qualification for that role is that they share Ministers' prejudices. What the Government wants is that nothing should intervene or mediate between itself and 25,000 primary and secondary schools, seen as 25,000 small, autonomous competing businesses.

If the grant-maintained school 'revolution' takes the course which the Secretary of State intends, then most secondary schools and a 'significant proportion' of primary schools will have 'opted out' of their local authorities and into the control of the Secretary of State by 1996.

The political importance attached to what is still a very small fraction of the school system is evident in the obsessive references to grant-maintained status in the White Paper. The Government would clearly like to see Local Education Authorities disappear altogether. Lacking the nerve, or the honesty, to announce their abolition, it prefers to place them in a condition of terminal decline and to risk the chaos of a transitional period when responsibility will be shared between them and unelected regional offshoots of a Funding Agency appointed by the Secretary of State.

It might reasonably be asked why grant-maintained status is desirable if, in the words of the White paper, 'all schools now have the freedom under local management of schools to take decisions reflecting their own priorities and circumstances...', but that question mistakes the Government's purposes and avoids the major issues. For it is not the autonomy of schools which dominates the White Paper, but the centralisation or nationalisation of schooling.

As a *The Times* leader noted (29 July 1992), it makes no mention of those 'bonds that tie schools to their communities through local democracy'. Yet it is surely 'extraordinary that a Conservative Government should have such contempt for them and such faith in the rectitude of Whitehall planning'. Nor is there any recognition that the quality of education in one school may depend in part on its place in a network of interdependent schools, that schools may have more to gain from *co-operation* than from competition, that human and financial resources are being wasted on unnecessary competition, that the 'free play' of market forces is inappropriate to education, and that unrestrained institutional self-interest is no basis for creating an effective, humane and equitable educational system.

Yet institutional and individual self-interest is the mainspring of the 1993 Act. Government policy is driven by a faith in the beneficial outcomes of market forces which is impervious to arguments that 'open' competition between schools both contradicts the values which most schools seek to uphold, or to evidence that such competition is likely to work to the detriment of those already disadvantaged by the circumstances in which they live. An insistence on what is called 'rigorous' testing, against the warnings of those who understand the damage which publicising the outcomes of narrow, mechanistic sampling of pupils' performance can do, reflects an uncritical belief in the motivating effects of league tables on the quality of education. League tables based on raw test scores do not accurately reflect the 'value added' by the teaching, as opposed to other factors, and they must have as many losers as winners. Highly ranked schools are likely to attract even more pupils and thus enhance their position.

Apart from its peculiar notion that 'under-performing' schools can be turned around by being placed in the control of yet another unaccountable quango and under the direction of retired 'experts', the White Paper has nothing to say about what will happen to that 'common grounding' in essential knowledge and understanding which the National Curriculum supposedly guarantees even in schools low in their local league tables. Those schools may well be coping with greater difficulties than more socially favoured competitors, yet they will now lack any prospect of effective support from an LEA deliberately deprived of the capacity to provide it.

Though the rhetoric of the White Paper is about diversity, and the approved S-word is specialisation and not selection, the reality is a strategy for restoring selection and creating a hierarchy of schools and types of school in which the tiers are likely to become rapidly steeper and more strongly marked. Few outside those convinced that the survival of the fittest allows only the meritorious to flourish will share the Government's confidence that an education system left to market forces will produce the equality of esteem between schools, and equality of opportunity between children, to which it declares itself committed.

Although the Government has used the language of 'diversity' to woo support from minority ethnic groups, there is little evidence of a genuine commitment to their needs. Muslim leaders who have interpreted clauses of the White Paper as heralding state-funded Islamic schools on anything more than a token scale are likely to be disappointed. The statements on this point in the White Paper are highly tentative and even evasive.

In reality, the Government is much more committed to curriculum specialisation than cultural diversity. The chapter of the White Paper entitled 'Specialisation and Diversity in Schools' is almost entirely about specialisation. And, even on that theme, the Government has promised more than it intends to deliver. Although the legislation is to be 'drawn widely enough to encourage more schools to specialise in other fields too', the emphasis is firmly on technology and the need to 'equip young people with the technological skills essential to a successful economy'.

The rhetoric of specialisation and diversity is given an added appeal by the Government's assurance that it will not entail selection and hierarchy. It stresses specialisation rather than selection and tells us that it is not its intention either to encourage or to discourage applications to make schools selective. Yet to say that its emphasis is on encouraging parents to choose, rather than schools to select, is to ignore the reality of what happens, either overtly or covertly, when schools are massively oversubscribed. Indeed the Secretary of State has already, in July 1993, given approval to an opted out school to become selective, and was publicly rebuked by a judge for giving the public the impression that his decision reflected the wishes of the local community, when this was not the case.

Yet the White Paper assures us that 'the Government wants to ensure that there are no tiers of schools within the maintained system (*sic*) but rather parity of esteem between different schools, in order to offer parents a wealth of choice'. The impression given is that each school is to be judged on its specific character and on its merits, rather than as one of a hierarchically arranged series of 'types'. This is to ignore the history of English education and the Government's noticeable lack of commitment to the same policy for the private sector suggests that it knows only too well that markets create tiers. We firmly reject the notion that the market 'knows best', that it alone can establish values, give choice, offer diversity and solve all our problems.

A VISION OF THE FUTURE

There is no vision of the future in what the Government is offering, other than the view that the market will provide for it. Yet a vision of what the future may hold should be at the heart of planning. Children who are in school today will only be in their teens or early twenties when the 21st century dawns. With improved medical care some may even see out most or all of the coming century. Education is an important investment in the future both for individuals and their families, and for the whole of society. Alvin Toffler, the American futurologist, said that all education was a vision of the future and that failure to have such a vision was a betrayal of the nation's youth. It is worth basing our vision, therefore, on the best conjecture we can make about what kind of future faces young people, not on nostalgia for a falsely imagined Golden Age in the past, whether in the 19th century or the 1960s.

There has been frequent speculation about the 21st century. The gloomier predictions portray a world of massive unemployment, in which only a small percentage of society hold a job and the rest are dependent on them, turning to multi-channel television for comfort. The more optimistic forecast is for longer, healthier life, the end of dangerous, dirty and dreary jobs, more time for recreation and leisure, but also the emergence of a range of fulfilling opportunities to work with people rather than objects. High quality education can help shape the future.

During the 1970s and early 1980s some 2.5 million jobs disappeared from manufacturing industry in this country. Although the great majority were unskilled and semi-skilled, some were skilled craft jobs, and others were managerial and scientific. The difference between recent recessions and previous ones is that many of the lost jobs never came back, or if they did return, it was often in much modified form. A million or more of the unemployed have been under 25, creating a large underclass of young people who, even if they increase their skills, often cannot find jobs. We need a new drive for full employment to capitalise on young people's energy and ambition so that it is not channelled, through lack of opportunity, into anti-social behaviour. Among messages emerging from the roller coaster patterns of employment in recent years are the following:

- We are in the middle of a post-industrial revolution, but cannot yet see the outcome
- There will be fewer unskilled, barely skilled and semi-skilled jobs
- People in the 21st century may have to change their job several times
- There will be more employment in service and support of other people
- Long term unemployment is rising, as is the number of part-time and precarious jobs

Some of the changes in home and family life are also likely to be significant. In order to be a full citizen in the next century it will be necessary to be aware both of one's rights and obligations. There will be a premium on skill not only in work but in family and social life. Some degree of competence will be needed to enjoy the full range of recreation and leisure opportunities available, otherwise participants will be restricted to a limited number of passive activities. Those lacking essential skills can easily fall victim to the predators in society. Loan sharks flourish when people lack the reading skill to understand the document they are asked to sign, the number skill to work out the true implications of high percentage interest charges, or the self-confidence to resist persistent sales pressure.

The implication for education of these possible changes are clear. Pupils leaving school need a strong foundation of basic skill in literacy and numeracy, of this there is no doubt, but it will not, in itself, be sufficient. In addition to the fundamental competence in several aspects of arts and sciences which some thirteen years of education should give them, young adults will need a broader education to give them a firm grounding for the variety of work and social experiences they are likely to encounter. They will need imagination so they can shape their own future and not be dependent on passive spectating for entertainment; flexibility, to enable them to adapt to rapidly changing circumstances in work and in their family and social life; determination, so that they will persist in the face of adversity, wherever it may occur; a sense of responsibility to their fellows.

This powerful mixture of intellectual and personal traits can only be nurtured in an education system which begins early, so that lifelong habits of learning are established, recognises individual differences and needs, and is resourced to provide fair opportunities for all, not just a few. In the 21st century the ability to work collaboratively as a member of a team will be even more vital. Problems are solved and significant discoveries are increasingly made by teams of people. Pupils need to learn subject knowledge, but also to understand what they have learned and to apply it in real life, often as a member of a project team.

A blend of distinctive individualism and the capacity for harmonious co-operation will be essential. No team could have painted the Mona Lisa or composed Beethoven's Fifth Symphony, but no individual could have sent someone to the moon. The next century will require both individual inspiration and the expert term approach shown by the American aerospace industry, which brings together leading experts on rocket technology, food and health in space, the fabrics of astronauts' clothing and the calculation of flight paths.

In family and social life, citizens of the next century will not only need to know about their rights and entitlements, but also be aware of their obligations to others. Ignorance about rights and obligations impedes people from playing a full part as citizens of their communities. Preparation for the 21st century involves the acquisition of knowledge, skills, attitudes and appropriate patterns of behaviour. In order to be healthy, for example, it is important to know about the causes of ill health, particularly those illnesses that are avoidable. However, knowledge in itself is insufficient, for unless people have the necessary skills to take proper exercise, look after their body, follow a healthy diet, adopt positive attitudes and actually behave in a healthy manner, little will be achieved.

There is another important aspect of the future that must be considered in any shaping of education policy. Compared with life in the 19th century, what are sometimes called the 'Four Ages' have changed dramatically. The First Age, the age of full-time education and training, has grown longer. For much of the last century this was short, or had ceased by the age of ten for most children. Today the First Age lasts at least eighteen years for the majority. As a consequence of this lengthening and the trend towards earlier retirement, the Second Age, the age of employment, has grown shorter. The present generation may retire at 55 or 60, and the Second Age may be thirty to forty years, not the half century or more of yesteryear.

It is uncertain whether a flexible retirement age may alter this position, but in any case the Third Age, the age of healthy retirement, grows longer with improved medical care. Indeed, many of the children in school today may enjoy thirty or forty years in the Third Age, an opportunity denied to their grandparents. Even the Fourth Age, the age of infirmity, makes demands on educational provision.

The inescapable consequence of this significant shift towards the lengthening of the Third Age in particular is a much higher priority for community education, the availability of high quality education and training for all, whether for those who have to retrain several times in their career, or for people eager to learn a foreign language or new hobby in middle age, or for the elderly. In future school education must be seen as a foundation for those who wish to learn throughout their lives, in whatever circumstances. The notion that education ceases for most people at the end of adolescence is increasingly outdated.

The challenges facing those responsible for educating generations who will live most of their lives in the 21st century are formidable. The demands on young adults have escalated in recent years and there is no sign that they will diminish, indeed the pace of accelerated demand is likely to be at least sustained if not increased. Citizens of the 21st century may need to be vastly more proficient in many aspects of their lives than was ever necessary in the 20th century.

It is no insult to teachers, therefore, to say that there will need to be a very significant increase in what children achieve during their schooling. Indeed in a period of rapid change teachers are among the most important members of society, and it is important to secure their enthusiastic commitment and collaboration, rather than alienate them, as has happened in recent years. Any attempt to educate all citizens effectively, whatever their age, wherever they live, irrespective of wealth, status or origin, would fail without the expertise and support of skilled teachers.

Developments in educational technology will also play an increasingly valuable role in this challenge to educate all citizens effectively. Radio, television, a range of printed materials and other aids to learning have played an important part in education throughout the last few years, but there are several attractive features of newer technology that offer even more promise. The development of the micro-computer showed that the machinery for teaching and learning could be much more individualised.

The interactive videodisc, with its vast storage and retrieval facilities and compact form, will increasingly become a powerful tool for teaching and learning, for massive multi-media libraries can be stored on just a handful of compact discs. The development and refinement of 'Virtual Reality', at present known as a three dimensional game environment, will offer considerable potential to those unable to attend learning institutions. A source of electrical power and a telephone link are all that is necessary to give someone access to the largest stocks of knowledge anywhere in the world.

Above all, however, education must also present to pupils a set of ideals, a way of living in which learning matters, a belief that the world can become a better place through their efforts. Education should enable all children and adults, according to age, ability and aptitude, to improve the quality of their lives through the development of their intellect and imagination.

Preparing young people for the uncertainties of the future is one of the most significant challenges facing us as the 20th century draws to a close. It is a challenge we must strive to meet. We must unite behind a crusade to empower all our citizens to develop their competence, to nurture the intellectual and personal knowledge, skills, attitudes and behaviour necessary for the next century, and to provide the high quality buildings, equipment and teachers necessary to achieve these goals. We fail at our peril.

THE VALUES AND PRINCIPLES OF EDUCATION

Recent Government education policy has espoused the language and values of a free trading market. There is emphasis on choice, particularly parental choice. Parents, on behalf of their children, are seen to be the 'consumers' of education. Education is considered as a 'commodity' within a service industry, within which parents pick and choose. Although it is not yet to be bought and sold in quite the same way as commodities within retail chains, 'education' is taking on many such features. Thus, the following assumptions are made:

- The consumer is thought to know best. As the White Paper, *Choice and Diversity,* put it, 'parents know best the needs of their children - certainly better than educational theorists or administrators, better even than our mostly excellent teachers'.

- To give consumers opportunity for exercising their preferences, a range of goods needs to be provided. Therefore, the White Paper argued for a diversity of provision - schools reflecting local circumstances, regional priorities, parental preferences and children's needs. Differences in provision have been established to enhance consumer choice through Grant Maintained as well as LEA schools, Assisted Places in the private sector, City Technology Colleges, and specialist schools amongst the Grant Maintained.

- For the consumer to exercise choice rationally, the differences in quality and taste need to be clearly marked. The most significant aspect of the National Curriculum has been the provision of pegs on which to hang a system of national assessment which enables the commodity (education), offered at each school, to be first measured and then labelled to help the consumers make their choices.

* For the consumer to *make*, rather than to dream about, choices, the means of choosing have to be provided. Voucher schemes have been rejected, but open enrolment and the parental right to choose, together with the Assisted Places Scheme, have, in theory, opened all schools to every parent who wishes to send children there.

The two principal beliefs are, therefore, that the consumer knows best and that he or she, not the professional educator, determines, through the exercise of choice, where children should be taught, and secondly that, even where the consumer has limited control over the ends to be achieved, the need for the producer and seller to attract the consumer means that only the best quality will survive. Competition keeps retailers on their toes.

We question this analysis, believing that it is fundamentally flawed both in the assumptions of how society functions and in the moral values which it promotes.

Freedom for some can mean less freedom for the rest. If some of us want our children to be in a class of fifteen, then other people's children might have to be in a class of forty to make up for it. Schools, in becoming selective, open up choices for some parents and close them to others. Grant Maintained Schools, in favouring some parents in their respective admissions policies, close their doors to other parents who, being in that neighbourhood, would otherwise wish their children to attend the school. Or, again, the public money put into City Technology Colleges (£100m in capital costs for the first fourteen) makes more choices available for the few, but thereby impoverishes the choices for the many. This aspect of freedom has received no attention in recent policy. There are important differences between 'making' and 'getting' your choice of school. Covert selection by over-subscribed schools, exploding rates of exclusion and expulsion and numbers of appeals (together with the Government's stated intention of removing spare capacity from the system) point to large numbers of parents being frustrated in the education market place. Many schools now see it in their interest to refuse or discourage children with special educational needs or to redistribute their resources in favour of those students most likely to perform well in GCSE examinations and National Tests.

Schools are seen to offer a service to individuals who seek their own personal betterment. It is the consumer who decides, and clearly the consumers will have an eye to what is in it for them. But schools should not, whilst in receipt of public money, have such a narrow and selfish purpose. What is taught, the values that are promoted, the relationships that are established, are geared as much to the public good as they are to private fortune, and it would be naive to see public good as simply the natural consequence of each pursuing his or her own private benefit. Schools aim to produce virtuous citizens as well as successful entrepreneurs. The *system* of education cannot reflect the sum of individual choices; it must also promote the values of our common humanity. Furthermore, the development of competition by the application of market forces to education has the effect of destroying co-operative and collegial relationships - suspicion, hostility and opportunism are encouraged. Shrewdness is rewarded, altruism and cooperation are penalised. In so far as students learn values through the community as well as in schools, the current market system may offer a good 'education' in entrepreneurism, but it is unlikely to transmit or enhance a model of positive social ethics.

Moreover, there has been total impoverishment of the language of education. Education is not a commodity to be bought or sold; it is a transaction that takes place between teacher and learner.

Pupils (or parents) are not consumers; they participate in that conversation which takes place between the generations of mankind in which they are introduced to the voice of poetry, of science, of history, of politics. The authorities in this conversation are not parents, as the Secretary of State would have it, but those who, from within an educational tradition so disparaged by the Government, are called upon to initiate the next generation into the achievements of literature and of history and into the wonders of scientific enquiry, as well as encouraging them to play their own part in that continuing process. The teacher of science is handing on to young people the accumulated wisdom and expertise of hundreds of years of scientific enquiry, as well as encouraging them to play their own part in the continuing process. The teacher of history is not responding to consumer whim or fancy, but providing an historical perspective from which the present might be understood and appraised.

The White Paper was trapped in an inadequate language of consumerism and an impoverished social philosophy of choice. It missed the distinctive aim of education and the distinctive role of schools. Above all, it subverted the role of the teacher which is to introduce the next generation to a culture that is much more than the sum of consumer choices, and to the critical tools through which those choices might be assessed and (if needs be) found wanting. We argue for a different set of values to which traditionally education has attached importance, and which meet a richer, more defensible view of human nature and human society.

In promoting an alternative philosophy we wish first of all to underline a set of values that should lie at the centre of any education system. Such principles as fairness and co-operation should be given prominence. The 1944 Education Act recognised the right of *all* children, irrespective of socio-economic background, ethnicity, religion, or personal qualities, to be educated according to age, ability and aptitude. Too often the much cherished freedom of the consumer is contrasted with equality. That would be valid if equality were to be synonymous with drab uniformity or with the neglect of individual differences. But equality refers to the principle of fairness - of not denying access to educational opportunity on grounds of wealth or social status or economic standing. Equality refers to the respect due to all pupils, as persons worth educating irrespective of background or individual quirks. Educational provision must justify differences of treatment, in so far as these differences affect the quality of life. Such justification would rest on educational considerations, not on privileged position or wealth. A *system* of education, in promoting equality, seeks not uniformity, but arrangements in which judgement of educational need is not determined by the capacity to manipulate the market in consumer-led provision.

Second, the parent and child should be respected not as consumers of a commodity but as contributors to a continuing debate about the purposes of education within a democratically accountable system. Democracy must not be limited to the signalling of idiosyncratic choices; it requires an informed and critical public. Certainly democracy entails freedom, but there are different meanings of the word 'freedom'. There is freedom from constraint - being able to do what one wants to do. But there is, too, freedom to *do* - having the intellectual capacity and personal qualities to live a distinctively human life. We stress equality and freedom in the important senses too long ignored, namely, a fair and just system of education in which *all* young people are freed from the constraints of ignorance and empowered to exercise critical and well informed judgement.

Third, a democratically accountable system should recognise the interdependence of people and the social richness on which each individual draws. We reject the prevailing 'official' view of society as an aggregate of individuals, constrained only by the regulations of the state. The relations between people, the civil context within which they live and work, the institutions which govern their lives, are as much a part of the human condition as are individual actions and choices. Indeed, the latter are inevitably rooted in the former. We need to move beyond the 'thin' and self-interested politics of elected parent governors voting to 'opt out'. Schools should be a part of and accountable to local communities.

Fourth, we reject competition as the sole motivating force in education. Some elements of competition may be necessary, even enjoyable if in the spirit of fairness and friendliness, but since most of adult life is based on collaboration, within the family, in the work place and community, the ability to live and work co-operatively with fellow adults and children will be an important element of life in the 21st century, if the social disasters of the 20th century are to be avoided.

We provide an alternative agenda to that of *Choice and Diversity*, because we believe that the stress upon individual choice ignores salient features of humanity - and of being fully human within society. By contrast, therefore, we place at the very centre of educational aims the capacity to be free - the freedom that arises from knowledge, understanding and personal integrity, not the false freedom of untrammelled consumerism. In promoting this freedom we insist upon a fair and just system which respects all children, not just those who, for one reason or another, exercise choice at the expense of others.

POWER AND STRUCTURE IN THE EDUCATIONAL SYSTEM

The National Curriculum was aimed to empower the State to 'direct' learning in pursuit of its economic and social goals. In the 1992 White Paper the Secretary of State argued that the principle of a national curriculum is no longer a matter of debate, except over its details. In one sense this is true. Once Parliament had given the Secretary of State enormous statutory powers to determine the structure and content of the curriculum there was little left for the citizenry to do but to 'debate' the details. Even here the empowering of the State through the 1988 Education Act has ensured a very loaded debate indeed, with little pretence on the part of the Government that it is seeking to negotiate a consensus with the various groups claiming a legitimate interest in the education of the nation's children. Views contrary to the ideological predispositions of the Government and personal prejudices of the Secretary of State and a few advisers are simply ignored, because there is no *statutory* obligation to accommodate them in the policy formation process.

In the 'debate' surrounding the principle of the National Curriculum, the assumption that the interests of the nation are synonymous with those of the Government was rarely questioned. Both advocates and opponents tended to interpret the principle of the National Curriculum as a form of 'State-led adjustment' (to use David Marquand's phrase) to the educational system. What was missing was any alternative interpretation of who should exercise power over children's learning. Ministers have disdained key constituencies. Neither democratically elected local politicians nor representatives of parents seem to have any real power or influence. LEA officers and local councillors were enraged by the Secretary of State failing to make his customary address to the North of England conference in January 1993, and the National Association of Parent-Teacher Associations were similarly distressed at his refusal to discuss the Key Stage 3 testing arrangements with them.

National representatives of interest groups have acted on the presumption that in a democracy they are entitled to be consulted because their views are relevant to the national interest, what Marquand called a 'negotiated adjustment' to the educational system. It is an interpretation which assumes that the national interest must be based on a synthesis which accommodates diverse sectional interests and presumes a degree of power sharing in the policy making process.

The 1988 Education Act, by giving the Secretary of State hundreds of additional powers, has allowed him to ignore any presumptions of power sharing and the right to consultation on the part of interest groups. John Patten has been accused of being an 'invisible man' for his refusal to listen to the views of interest groups. But his conduct should not be personalised in this way, for such portrayals simply divert attention away from the fact that it is conduct consistent with the powers bestowed on him by the 1988 Act. Any redistribution of those powers would require a new act of Parliament to establish policy making structures that guarantee the entitlement of different interest groups to participate in a debate about the form and content of the National Curriculum.

Such a debate would not be a one-off event or series of events, like the so-called 'consultation exercises' which routinely accompany the publication of Government proposals. In his book, *Take Care, Mr Baker!*, Julian Haviland analysed all 11,790 responses to the Government's consultation paper on the 1988 Bill and concluded that every single one expressed reservations about the National Curriculum. The warning messages were ignored. Peremptory ministerial decree has replaced debate, consultation and negotiation.

David Marquand's distinction between 'state-led' and 'negotiated' adjustments to social systems arises out of a context where the structure of Britain's political institutions increasingly fails to accommodate the interests of significant groups in society. In these circumstances state-imposed policies lose legitimacy for significant proportions of the citizenry who are powerless to change them. Even the apparently democratic process of local and general elections may fail to empower such groups when the procedures shaping them assume that politics is a competitive struggle between parties for a majority vote rather than, as is the case in many European countries, a more consensual process of power-sharing between a diversity of political and social interest groups.

Power sharing implies that state-led policy making will include negotiated adjustments. The reform of our political institutions in this country to enable the integration of consensus within the organs of the State may be a future possibility, but in the short-term we must seek the election of a Government that is persuaded of the wisdom of devolving some of its 'sovereign powers' over policy making by establishing dialogue with its citizenry and not assuming a monopoly of wisdom.

The reasons for establishing power-sharing structures are quite simple. The history of state-led social planning, which ignores the concerns of those it affects, gives few grounds for optimism on the part of the planners. The outcomes they seek to engineer remain unrealised, because any significant social change requires the voluntary co-operation of those affected by it. This can only be achieved by shifts in outlook and attitude that emerge within a process of unconstrained debate between the interested parties. The use by the state of an engineering model of social planning, exemplified in the National Curriculum and other structural changes the Government has initiated in education, may well be an effective means of disempowering significant political and social groups in society, such as LEAs, educational researchers, parents' associations, inspectors, even employers' associations and employees' unions - but it is very ineffective in achieving a level of co-operation beyond that of passive compliance.

Quality in education depends upon the commitment of all interested parties to realising a common vision, a vision which transcends but accommodates diversity of outlook, and which is constructed out of painstaking dialogue, rather than imposed from above. The engineering model embodies a mechanical view of power as a force to be applied to malleable material. But the human race can construct cultures through association - shared outlooks and attitudes - which, as recent events in Russia and Eastern Europe have shown, are highly resistant to the use of coercive power by the State. Cultural change - involving shifts of attitude and outlook - is a necessary condition of any worthwhile social change, and it is brought about when members of a culture are able to take part in genuine and open debate.

The creation of the National Curriculum and the restructuring of the system according to market assumptions, provides no coherent vision of education as a common good. It leaves no space for citizens - as parents, teachers, employers, employees - to construct a vision together with the Government. In place of debate the imposition of a crude social market will, as we have argued above, produce an unfair society, where a few have the power of choice and the less affluent, less influential, are denied it, resulting in all manner of inequalities and injustices within the system. Even the Government's selection of content within the National Curriculum is shaped by an outmoded nationalism which ignores the realities of our multi-cultural society and the increasing inter-dependence of nations. It thus appeals to those who refuse to wake up to the realities of social change by re-examining their traditional beliefs and attitudes.

In denying the citizenry its right to participate in the educational policy debates, the Government acts in a totalitarian manner. Just as Marxist-Leninism legitimated the power of states behind the iron curtain, so the social market provides a superficially sophisticated device for the exercise of state power to transform traditional social democracies. The social market enables the state to masquerade in democratic disguise while systematically undermining democracy.

What is required is a new power-sharing structure to support the democratic participation of the citizenry in educational policy-making. The interests of children, their parents, teachers (through the proposed General Teaching Council and Teacher's Professional Associations), employers and employees, need to be represented in policy debates and decisions operating at national, local/regional, and school levels. What should be interlocking, rather than confrontational interests of central and local government, need to be represented. Both central and local government should be required to share power with those groups in society that have a legitimate interest in the aims and processes of education in our schools. Government-nominated quangos alone cannot achieve this, but genuine debate and consultation between democratically elected local and national representatives and groups interested in and concerned with education, would have a better chance of success. As the 21st century dawns, we can no longer trust the adversarial system of party politics operating in both central and local government to help us share power in a fair and just manner.

THE ORGANISATION OF EDUCATION

The draining away of responsibility from local education authorities and towards individual schools and the Government itself has left a vacuum at local and regional level. At national level committees and quangos have been packed with members sympathetic to the Government's point of view. The assumption at local level is that all schools should opt out and then compete as autonomous businesses. Matters like the provision of school places, the education of children with special needs, co-ordination and co-operation amongst schools, further professional training for teachers, group trading, quality control, and non-statutory education, are thus left largely to the market.

At national level any committees to do with curriculum, assessment, the training of teachers, or other matters to do with education should be fully representative of the various interests, teachers, parents, governors, employers, members of the education service and of the community at large. There can be no better model of impartiality than that which was properly encouraged at local level in the reform of the composition and functions of governing bodies required by the 1986 (No. 2) Education Act. The exclusive appointment of politically nominated members to national and local bodies should cease.

Four yearly inspections are too frequent where schools are known to be improving, but insufficient to act as a proper spur to improvement when schools are in decline. A better model would involve schools themselves carrying out a self-review against agreed criteria over a five year period on different aspects of school life, with an external ingredient in each such review. There would be proper provision for a full external review and inspection when a new head is appointed, because schools at that point are expecting to move in new directions as the newly appointed leader produces a development plan. Such choices will be the better informed when they are dependent not merely on his/her view of the school but also that of others. If no change occurs within a seven year time span, then a full inspection should take place to avoid any sense of complacency developing, which can sometimes happen with the long service of a single headteacher.

An Education Authority or Council which is democratically accountable at local level seems to us to be the best vehicle to ensure that sound programmes are pursued. There is a clear link in any case between the development of education and democracy. In a population as large as that of the U.K., moreover, it seems unlikely that the necessary sense of common purpose and detailed sensitive adjustment of detail is best achieved solely at a national level. This raises questions about the role of such a locally elected Authority. One possibility is to decide that education is such an important service to the whole community that members of any Authority responsible for it should be directly elected, rather than nominated from within the overarching City or County Councils. This would be a contentious matter, so it should be fully debated. The alternative is to keep Local Education Authorities but change their role. They should certainly be required to work much more closely with the departments responsible for social services, health, recreation and leisure, and housing than has often been the case previously, if coherent programmes responsive to the needs of the community are to be initiated and sustained.

We have grave doubts that the funding agencies suggested by the Government for opted out schools will be responsive to parents or to local needs. Indeed the Government's arrangements for setting up and running grant maintained schools seems to establish a bureaucracy unaccountable to local opinion, as well as to be a recipe for unfairness. In the same way that parents have been wrongly encouraged to think that they can have limitless choice, so the grant maintained schools falsely appear to be independent, yet face substantial liability to controls from the new Funding Agency appointed by the Secretary of State. As in so many matters the Secretary of State becomes prosecutor, judge and jury. That is incompatible with a healthy democracy.

We believe that all schools in an area should have a high degree of self-management, but they should be subject to local democratic accountability for general planning and take advantage of an LEA managed admission system. The LEA would plan the system and have its general plans approved by the Secretary of State. There would, however, be an important difference from what has happened in the past, with no return to the overbearing and bureaucratic interference of some LEAs in school matters. Moves to greater delegation and decision making over the disposition of monies, first pioneered in Local Education Authorities, and then enshrined in law through schemes of local management, would remain. These moves have been generally welcomed in principle and mostly in practice. Reservations have been expressed about the detailed nature of the national regulations governing the schemes, including a dogmatic approach to the treatment within the formula of the cost of teachers' salaries, which has led to some schools having to make experienced teachers redundant in order to balance their books. This system should end and a more equitable distribution of resources devised which does not penalise schools with older teachers.

The future functions of LEAs should include the following:

- The co-ordination of parental choices and school admissions and across networks of schools

- The provision of expert advice and school inspection and support for changes recommended as a result of inspection

- The provision of services, as well as being charged with securing goods and services from the best source, whilst not being a monopoly provider

- Helping schools co-ordinate the continuity of curriculum planning across the various phases of education through academic councils, both during and beyond the compulsory years of schooling

- The provision of extra help for those with special educational needs

- The continuing professional development of teachers and other personnel

- Maintaining and enhancing the education of the whole community. (Although the colleges of further education, former polytechnics, colleges of higher education and older universities are independent of local authorities, LEAs should still keep under review the opportunities for education for everyone in the city or county, in partnership with the providers.)

ACCOUNTABILITY IN EDUCATION

That the education system should be accountable is a general principle to which most people can subscribe. Some features of accountability, for example financial ones, are relatively straightforward to define, at least in principle. The more difficult features are those which relate to the purposes of institutions, such as to foster the learning or general development of those individuals (or other institutions) for which they have assumed a limited responsibility. We focus here in particular on institutions whose aim is to promote learning, namely schools and colleges of various kinds, on the Government's narrow view of 'value for money', and on the matter of school inspection.

The first, crucial, point is that a school can only take responsibility, and hence credit, for *some* of the learning which takes place within it. A great deal of learning, both academic and non-academic, takes place outside schools and colleges; in homes, in contact with the media, and in general human relationships. The difficulty lies, therefore, in separating out the contribution of the institution from that of other contributors. This can only be done with a certain degree of accuracy and depends crucially for its success on correctly identifying and accounting for both sets of factors, those external and those internal to the school.

All the relevant research supports the view that the results of such exercises yield comparisons between institutions which are indicative but not descriptive. That is, they suggest which institutions may be performing well above or well below the level expected of them, but, because of the inherent uncertainties of the comparisons, these cannot simply be labelled as 'poor' or 'good'. In other words, the function of such comparisons should be that they are used as a screening device, to be handled with caution.

As a screening instrument, however, comparisons between schools can be of value. They can direct the attention of schools, or departments within them, to possible areas of deficiency which may require reorganisation or the provision of extra resources. They can also direct attention to those institutions which appear to be relatively successful, so that lessons can be learnt. Important information may be gained about why certain children seem to prosper in some schools while others do not.

The issue may be put another way. We sometimes discover, from comparisons, that some institutions are performing better than others. What we cannot do is identify with precision just which those institutions are. In some cases this may be because the number of students within an institution is too small to produce an accurate estimate, in other cases because there is a variation from year to year which cannot be accounted for. This uncertainty principle can be recognised when making comparisons by placing limits, typically wide, around the position of each institution in rank order. In the present state of understanding there is no case for using the results of such accountability exercises in a systematic way directly to determine such factors as remuneration, promotion or funding. Nor should they be taken by users of the educational system, such as parents and students, as providing 'hard' evidence about the worth of any particular institution. We believe that the promotion of such ideas as crude league tables in the Government's 'Parents' Charter' is misleading and inimical to the pursuit of well informed choice.

Nothing we have said suggests that measures of accountability should be withheld from public scrutiny. Some schemes for comparing schools are based upon the view that only individual institutions should have access to the information. That seems to us a limited approach and cannot truly provide public accountability. The difficulty lies in deciding which information is worth publicising and who is to make such a decision. There is a need for a national body, independent of the institutions themselves and of government, backed up by relevant technical expertise, and perhaps directly accountable to Parliament. Such a body would have responsibility for advising on the usefulness of particular measures and the desirability of research and development. It would have a particular responsibility for seeing that any proposals are properly piloted and evaluated before and during their implementation, something the School Examinations and Assessment Council did not always ensure.

There are several basic issues involved in providing measures of institutional performance which should be underlined. First, it is necessary, when measuring 'outputs' of any institutions to take into account their respective 'inputs'. The success of institutions can be judged only by how far the students in them make progress, the so called 'value added' by the system. Secondly, institutions will not in general be expected to enhance the progress of all their students to the same degree. Not only will there be differences between departments in the same institution, there will also be institutions in which relatively 'low' achievers make a great deal of progress but relatively 'high' achievers do not, and *vice versa*.

Some schools will encourage, through their organisation and curricular structure, the progress, say, of particular minority groups more than others. The practical difficulty lies in collecting information which will explain how this happens. The imposition of Key Stage testing of 7, 11, 14 and 16 year olds will do little to assist the process, since there is to be no collection of 'contextual data', so we will have no details of the personal background of the students or their families.

Nothing in the present Government's plans suggests that they have understood these issues. Their proposals to continue publishing 'league tables' of examination results at the ages of 11 and 16 are tendentious in intent and may delude people into thinking that the information they contain says anything reliable about the quality of education in the institutions listed. Crude unadjusted league tables are simply misleading and there are no grounds for publishing them as indicators of quality.

The inspection of individual schools should, in theory at any rate, allow for a form of accountability that takes contextual factors into the reckoning. However, the privatisation of school inspection has done little to improve the system of accountability, other than establish a regular cycle of inspection, which is to be welcomed. The recruitment of free-lance inspectors, working for profit, trained in a week in a hotel, has deprofessionalised school inspection. The unrefined, league table, performance indicator approach to inspection, whereby lightly trained inspectors apply simple quantitative measures, like truancy figures, to their scrutiny of education, will tell us little about the real story of succeeding and failing schools. The only redeeming feature is the presence in such teams, in the short term at least, of people with a background in LEA or HMI school evaluation, but this cannot be guaranteed in the longer term.

Since the new style of inspection is divorced from advice (inspection is a business, so there is no point in going back voluntarily to a school to help it improve what it does, as this cuts back on the opportunities for further profits), it will be seen by schools as a punitive exercise. Indeed, the proposal to send in 'hit squads' of retired headteachers when schools are thought to be failing is another misunderstanding of how to assess and improve quality.

Much better would be a linked national and local system of inspection and advice, with Her Majesty's Inspectors, from their national perspective, liaising closely with locally based teams of inspectors and advisers. This would enable national and local concerns to be addressed in a sensitive and thoughtful manner, and for reports on schools and colleges to be followed up quickly with advice and further monitoring, where necessary, on a more continuous basis.

Alongside this service should be a vigorous programme of school self-review against agreed criteria and with an external ingredient. Teacher appraisal should be an important part of this continuing process, but the emphasis should be on support and development. If some teachers are incompetent, the appropriate action should be taken, but appraisal should be based on the assumption that most teachers are willing to work positively at their professional skills, not on the supposition that most are incompetent. When a new head is appointed there should, wherever possible, be a full external review, so that decisions about change are well informed. Inspection should be a continuing and stable service, part of an open, honest, rational and public form of accountability, not a source of private entrepreneurism, ruled by market forces and profit making.

The limitation of the Government's view of accountability is that it has put an immense premium on formal pencil and paper tests of a limited kind. Testing plays an important part in education, but no test on earth can provide all the necessary information on pupil learning, diagnosis of children's needs, information for parents, teachers and employers, assessment of the quality of teaching and learning, year on year, region by region or school by school. National standards of attainment are better measured by national sampling, such as has been done by the Assessment of Performance Unit, and the quality of what goes on in individual classrooms and schools by both self-review and external appraisal.

PUBLIC AND PRIVATE PROVISION OF EDUCATION

The distinction between public and private provision of education is not a simple one. For the purposes of this paper we shall use the following terms to describe the new pattern of schooling that is emerging:

Maintained Schools: those maintained by the Local Education Authority (LEA) and those maintained by central government (Grant Maintained schools or GMS). Both LEA and GMS include voluntary aided and voluntary controlled schools - mainly Church schools in which the trustees own the premises and, through the Governing Bodies, exercise a great deal of control over appointments and admissions. 15% of capital costs of voluntary aided schools are paid for privately. Often maintained schools are referred to as state schools but that is mistake because the state does not own them even though it controls the curriculum.

Private Schools: those schools which, even though registered under Section 70 of the 1944 Education Act, are independent of central and local government in that their main resource is not provided by government, and they are not subject to the same legal requirements, including those of the National Curriculum. There are currently 235 Headmasters Conference or HMC schools, and 29 'market leaders' in the Eton and Harrow group, which, because recruitment is economically and socially selective and conditional upon certain levels of academic performance, gives a one-sided view of the total picture. The private sector is extremely diverse and totals 2,287 schools (1991 figures). It includes, in addition to the HMC schools, lesser-known boys' schools, 268 girls' schools within the Girl's Schools Association (including the fairly prestigious 26 schools within the Girls' Public Day Schools Trust), mixed schools even within HMC, about 550 preparatory schools, special schools (including the

Rudolph Steiner), religious schools (including Roman Catholic, Anglican, Jewish, 15 Islamic and an 'all-black' Seventh Day Adventist), the Atlantic College and a European School, the Montessori schools, a number in the 'small schools' movement and, since the 1988 Act, the City Technology Colleges (CTCs). Cutting across these distinctions is that between schools with charitable status and 'non-charitable' profit-making schools.

The distinction between 'private' and 'maintained' is increasingly blurred as maintained schools depend on private sponsorship and private schools receive public financial support. Some schools within the so-called independent sector are increasingly *dependent* on public funds.

Sixth-form, Tertiary and Further Education Colleges cannot be omitted from this overall picture of the 'school system' because many students transfer to them from both maintained and private schools to continue their full-time studies at the age of 16. As a result of the 1992 Further and Higher Education Act, these colleges have become corporate bodies, maintained no longer by the LEAs but out of public funds distributed through the Further Education Funding Council. However, though publicly funded in the main, they are expected to cover the cost of much of their work through fees and through various competitive measures. They interestingly straddle the private/public domains.

In 1991 the number of students in the private sector was just under 8% of the 5 to 18 full-time school and college population compared to just under 6% in 1979. The proportion of 5 to 10 year olds in independent education increased by more than 10% between 1981-87. The number of single sex schools has declined as has that of schools with boarding pupils only.

The educational reforms of the 1980s, particularly the 1988 Education Act, has fudged the distinction between the private and the maintained sectors of education. These reforms established a quasi-market within the maintained sector of education, and between that and the private sector, through (ostensibly) greater parental choice of schools, by subsidisation of private schools and by part privatisation of the maintained sector. In effect, schools in the maintained sector now resemble private schools much more - marketing their institutions, managing resources, deciding on priorities for spending, attracting clients, seeking sponsorship and other sources of funding, and acting competitively, without the LEA strategic planning within which, until recently, they had operated.

There are three reasons in particular why the distinction is increasingly difficult to sustain:

- **The Private Investment in Maintained Education**

    The 1944 Education Act established that everyone should be educated from 5 to 16 according to age, ability and aptitude, not according to private means. But, as schools succeed, so will aspirations grow and there will be increasing demands upon the maintained sector which it may not be able to meet. Therefore, despite the ideals of the 1944 Act, there is an increasing dependence upon private means, even for what many headteachers regard as essentials. Indeed, it was estimated by the *Directory of Social Change* in 1991 that private fund-raising might be contributing over £150m per year to meet basic costs.

    Some teaching posts within the maintained sector are now providing by private sponsorship or supported by parental fund-raising. Such examples are not, according to NFER research, isolated cases, but at the moment the extent is difficult to quantify. The point is, however, that this will probably increase under industrial sponsorship of maintained schools and a declining financial base.

There are various ways in which schools raise this money: commercial sponsorship, money raising events such as jumble sales, covenanting and (for over 10% of primary schools, according to the NFER research) levies of a 'voluntary fixed amount' - fees in all but name. The National Confederation of Parent Teacher Associations noted in 1991 that PTAs are being asked to contribute to essential class resources. This is likely to be a continuing trend under Local Management of Schools (LMS).

- **The Public Investment in Private Education**

Private schools are expensive and fee increases during the 1980s rose well above the rate of inflation. Fees for full boarders in 1993 are in some schools well over £10,000. Public money is contributed to private schools in the following ways:

(a)　**Assisted Places Scheme (APS)**
In 1980 the Assisted Places Scheme made available up to 6,000 means tested places to 'academically able' children whose parents could not afford full private school fees. By 1991, this had risen to about 30,000. An evaluation of the scheme reported in 1991 that the places are predominantly taken up by the 'submerged middle class' rather than widening the social class recruitment.

(b)　**Charitable Status**
Private schools receive financial support through their charitable status. As charities the schools qualify for a variety of tax concessions, including exemption from income tax, corporation tax, capital gains tax and VAT.

(c)   **National and Local Government payment of fees**

Often a condition of employment in Government overseas service (civil and foreign service or the military) is that the children should be educated in the UK, and in many cases these children are placed in private boarding schools such that these become an important source of public revenue. LEAs place many pupils with behavioural or learning difficulties in special schools which are outside the maintained sector. An Aided Places Scheme supports private music and ballet schools.

(d)   **City Technology Colleges (CTCs)**

CTCs are classified as private schools. They were established initially with a view to gaining industrial sponsorship for schools which normally would be maintained. In fact, such sponsorship was not forthcoming on any significant scale; industry by and large preferred to work with all schools, not a privileged minority. Consequently, the Government stepped in where commerce feared to tread. The first 14 CTCs cost the Treasury £100 million in capital costs.

(e)   **Training Credits**

Until recently FE Colleges were maintained by LEAs and provided the education and training, usually on a part-time basis, for young employees who were acquiring operative, craft, commercial and technological qualifications. FE Colleges have now become much more open (or vulnerable) to market forces, depending on 'clients' to remain viable. This is reflected particularly in the recent development of credits. Training credits, which carry a monetary value, give young people who have left full-time education the power to 'buy' training in approved maintained or private institutions and firms.

• **The Privatisation of Services within the Public Sector**

A new set of arrangements that brings independent and maintained sectors more closely together is the privatisation of services. Once, schools and colleges brought their resources from the public sector, they were cleaned, fed and serviced by the public sector. All that has changed as competitive tendering for most services is legally binding. The latest and most drastic measure concerns the privatisation of the inspection of schools, removing this responsibility from the LEAs, although leaving with HMI the crucial role of approving the new inspectors who will need to be trained to inspect.

To many people the developments we have outlined may be quite acceptable. Private schools bring in to the educational system as a whole over £1 billion of private money which otherwise would have to be found from the public purse; 'subsidising' such donations would seem to be only just. The able children of poor parents are said to receive opportunities from the private sector which otherwise would be denied them without public subsidy. The best private schools are said by some to provide a yardstick of good education which others might emulate. The more money conscious and 'market place' approach to education brings with it an awareness of the economic costs of this expensive service.

Nonetheless, there are problems which need to be addressed. No government could abolish independent schools, as this would arguably contravene the European Convention of Human Rights (Article 2 of the First Protocol to the Convention). Indeed, it would be wrong to deny parents the right to withdraw their children from what was publicly provided if they feel strongly about the quality of what is offered. But the provision of independent education is not just a private affair because it provides public leaders, it promotes public values and it indirectly shapes the future of society. There must be public responsibility for private education, and particularly its relation to the public sector which is affected by it and its use of assets which, directly or indirectly, benefit from public subsidy.

We recommend that:

- Charitable status, if preserved for private schools, should be extended to all

- Public funds assigned to schools should take into account the socio-economic factors which disadvantage certain schools in a competitive market

- Private schools, enjoying public funding, should be obliged to share resources with less advantaged maintained schools (e.g. playing fields, arts centres, science laboratories)

- There should be more experimental/alternative schools in the maintained system, as some of these exist solely or largely in the private sector.

- Independent schools, enjoying public funding, should:
    (i)   be more accountable to the taxpayer for aims, use of money and achievements

    (ii)   accept responsibility for many more children with special needs (including emotionally and behaviourally difficult children) which disproportionately are the responsibility of maintained schools

- The Government should recognise the potentially damaging consequences for schools as a whole in subjecting them to unfettered market forces - particularly maintained schools which are having to market themselves (and raise funds) locally

- The National Curriculum and National Assessment should be legally binding on *all* schools

- A clear statement should be made about the minimum funding required for *all* schools to meet the requirements of a broad and balanced curriculum.

PARENTS AND GOVERNORS

The two most significant lay constituencies in education, other than the public at large, are parents and governors. Both have seen their role changed markedly in the last decade. In 1989 John Tomlinson wrote that 'Parent are being asked to adopt a significantly new and difficult role in their relations with teachers. Research over the last generation has shown the advantages to children's education of their parents being involved as collaborators with teachers... Under the new proposals, parents are being asked to adopt the role of inquisitor and monitor of teachers and schools and to use new complaints procedures, all in the exercise of consumer sovereignty'.

Over the past four years parents have been pressed more and more to take the role of inquisitor, complainant, and vigilante, and to see themselves as consumers of education. The alternative policy is that parents should see themselves as joint producers of education with teachers, and should work in genuine partnership. The Government makes much of the way parents are to be used to create a market place in which 'choice' triggers competition between schools and thus improves standards as unpopular schools close. But many parents do not wish to embrace the new role in which they are cast. The National Confederation of Parent-Teacher Associations has rejected the idea of publishing league tables of examination results and has deplored the idea that parents should help to create competition between schools. Lord Taylor who chaired the 1977 Committee which produced *A New Partnership for our Schools* has written of the dismay many parents have expressed that education is being 'turned into a market place, where only the strong survive and that at the expense of their conscience'.

Parents have intuitively felt what research has suggested - that to educate all children to higher levels and raise standards for all, partnership not competition is the key. Any government really

concerned to raise standards will recognise that in future all
parents will need closer involvement with schooling. This will
mean:

- Giving parents more 'rights' to information about
  education than current legislation allows. A Freedom of
  Information Act should incorporate a section on parents'
  rights.

- A new legislative framework to ensure that all parents
  are involved in schools and can participate in decision-
  making. Parental support, involvement and obligation to
  participate in formal education will be part of new
  legislation for a more equal relationship between parents
  and teachers.

- The removal of the current powers of head teachers to
  prevent parents forming associations.

- One measure which parents do want and which the
  NCPTA was campaigning for long before the 1988
  Education Act has not been met in any charters. This is
  the right to set up home-school associations in schools,
  a measure which many parents think would bring homes
  and schools nearer to a genuine partnership.

England has for a long time lagged behind European neighbours
in legislating for parents' associations. In Germany all provinces
have a legal requirement for parent councils at all levels of
education - there are school class councils, district and provincial
parents councils. The provincial council offers advice to the
Minister of Education and must be kept informed by the
Minister. In France parent groups are funded by the Ministry and
have a legal right to be consulted. The Minister of Education
writes an official 'Letter to Parents'. All primary schools are
required to have a joint committee of teachers and parents.

The Danish school system is rooted in the idea of community education and gives more legal recognition and informed support to partnership between family and school than any other country. In the Danish basic school each school Board includes parents with voting rights as well as teachers and pupils. European countries have recognised that leaving home-school relations to voluntary co-operation does not work. If parental participation and partnership are to be a reality for all parents, formal participation at the class and school level, set within a legislative framework, is essential:

•   Home-school associations - of which all parents are automatically members, would be set up in every school.

•   The associations would be open to all parents, teachers and representative pupils, would be funded by a government grant and be part of a new legislative framework for homes and schools.

•   The associations would not be concerned with fund raising or social activities, they would be a forum for passing over knowledge and information about formal schooling to parents, and the passing of information on home learning to teachers.

•   The associations would discuss matters relating to children's learning, progress and achievement, curriculum, assessment, recording, teaching methods, behaviour in schools and school organisation.

•   The associations would include class associations as the main way to bring teachers and parents together. Parents would work with teachers to involve those parents who for practical or other reasons find it difficult to involve themselves with school. (This would reduce the complaint that 'the parents we really want to see never come').

• The associations would inform themselves of the professional services teachers offer, their rights, their conditions of service and their needs as a professional body.

• The associations would be statutorily consulted at local level when important decisions were being made on education, and representatives would be similarly consulted at national level. The associations would liaise with but not replace governing bodies.

• The associations would organise school publications and home-school communications, make arrangements for obligatory consultation above individual children, co-ordinate home-school learning schemes and homework arrangements and arrange parental involvement in day to day school activities.

• Written home-school parents' educational agreements (contracts) for every pupil would be developed within the framework of a home-school association.

Governors too have an important part to play in education. The Government has tended to give them powers, but not the support that such responsibilities need. Many governors have still had little or no training for their complex role. Their minimum entitlement should include:

• A proper induction programme so that new governors fully understand their powers and responsibilities from the outset.

- Further training as necessary for those who have already served for a year.

- Support from the government, not blame. Both anxiety and hostility were aroused when John Patten wrote a clumsy letter to governors which appeared to threaten them if teachers boycotted tests. Volunteer lay people should not be put under unfair political pressure.

SECTION 2

PRE-SCHOOL EDUCATION

In this country, the development of the pre-school sector during
the twentieth century has been *ad hoc*, resulting in a diversity in
the provision of care and/or education for the under fives.
Provision varies both in quantity and in quality, with wide
regional and local variations. There are differences of
environment, resources, length of sessions, training and
qualifications of adults/staff, and the curriculum offered. This
leads to significant variations in the quality of children's pre-
school experiences. Consequently there is increasing concern that
children are already unequally provided for by the age of five.

Responsibility for the three main sectors - statutory, voluntary
and private - straddles three government departments, Health,
Education and Social Services. The service providers all have
different priorities, objectives, philosophies and values.
Increasingly they are jousting with each other for a share of
diminishing resources. This has led to a situation where
fragmentation rather than co-ordination is the general rule which,
on the whole, tends to work against the interests of young
children and their families, rather than for them.

Three major themes recur in the debate about pre-schooling:
firstly, persistent under-funding and a lack of priority; secondly,
a commitment by recent Conservative Governments to increased
involvement by the private sector and an emphasis upon parental
responsibility for funding childcare; thirdly, demographic and
employment trends, which have created a market for childcare
support services where demand outstrips supply, with costs,
particularly in the private sector, proving prohibitive to low-
income families.

These trends are set against an expanding base of theory and knowledge of how young children learn, with broad agreement about appropriate curricula for this age group. The emphasis, in all settings, is on the need to provide care and education in a safe, stimulating environment with skilled, appropriately trained and knowledgeable adults. Research studies both here and in America also demonstrate the long-term benefits to children, their families and to society which accrue from participation in high quality pre-school education. From evaluations of the American Project Headstart onwards, the gains, particularly for children who might otherwise drop out or fall behind, have been significant, though not all persisted throughout school life. Research both in Britain and the United States has shown higher staying on rates, more college and vocational course participation, and other gains amongst groups who had good quality nursery education than amongst comparable groups who did not.

During the last five years there have also been three major government reports on the under fives, all of which have emphasised the need for improvements in both the quality and quantity of provision. However, lack of central funding means that the recommendations of these reports have been largely ignored. Similarly, the Children Act (1989) lays down statutory requirements for the registration and inspection of all pre-school settings. Again, lack of funding and of systems for co-ordination could result in a clipboard exercise where 'surface' features - space, adult-child ratios, number of toilets - are assessed but the quality of children's learning experiences is neglected. It is evident that in the pre-school sector, recent governments have been unable and unwilling to put cash and resources behind their own rhetoric.

Several fundamental issues need to be addressed if young children are to receive the high quality care and education which they need and deserve.

- Better co-ordination between providers. This requires the ending of entrenched interests and any one type of provider adopting a superior or territorial attitude. This can only be achieved through communication and co-operation towards agreed ends and with complementary means. Inter-agency and inter-professional training are a significant step forward, but changes in philosophy will be fundamental to changes in policy and practices.

- Liaison between different forms of pre-school provision and better continuity of experience for young children.

- Partnership between parents and service providers to ensure that the needs of both children and their parents are met.

- Liaison between home, pre-school and primary school with shared record keeping, better communication.

- Improved training. Currently there is a shortage not only of trained personnel in this field, but also of courses, and existing courses are inadequately funded. There should be a sharing of knowledge and expertise across the services in order to provide courses which equip adults for multi-disciplinary roles. Future training courses should be structured to enable progression, foster a greater degree of professionalisation, and enhance the status of those who work with the under fives. Training for early years teachers should include a multi-professional perspective, so that future practitioners are better able to influence or effect change (e.g. home/school links, liaison between settings, shared record keeping systems).

- Funding. It is difficult to see how the provision of high quality services for young children can be met without significant increases in funding in the statutory and voluntary sectors, or other incentives to employers and employees. If choice and diversity are to be raised from the realms of rhetoric into reality, then choices need to be made available to all families, regardless of income, and diversity should recognise and meet the needs of all children.

Fundamental to these developments is a shift in society's values. Current levels of provision and the fragmented nature of services for the under fives reflect the low status of young children in our society, and of the adults who work with them. As consumers of goods, children represent a lucrative market. As consumers of services they demand high investment with no promise of an immediate 'return'.

All those involved with young children, in whatever capacity, need to create a climate in which children and childhood really matter. The youngest children are the most vulnerable and least powerful members of society. They are further disempowered by those in authority who fail to acknowledge or understand the importance of the first five years. In addition to better systems and structures, children also need powerful advocates at all levels in society.

Better provision for young children is a question of social justice and of human rights. There is a danger in the present system that children who are already disadvantaged may be further disadvantaged, particularly those with special educational needs, or from ethnic minority groups, or already experiencing inadequate or inappropriate forms of provision. If equality for the under fives has been an elusive ideal in the past, then a greater degree of equity must be more than a vision for future generations. At the very least the promise of a nursery place for all three and four year olds whose parents wish it, made by Margaret Thatcher over 20 years ago, should now be fulfilled.

PRIMARY AND SECONDARY EDUCATION

The 1988 Education Act and subsequent legislation have moved responsibilities for decisions about primary and secondary schools away from the Local Education Authority, which used to act as a powerful broker, towards central government on the one hand and individual schools on the other. On matters like the local management of resources some initiative has been given to schools, but on crucial issues like the curriculum far too many powers have been taken by the Secretary of State, even down to decreeing what is taught and, increasingly, how it is taught. Decentralisation has devolved the task of reporting and recording outcomes, but retained and enhanced direct control by the Government over the fine detail of the curriculum, and so left it open to arbitrary interventions and sudden, disruptive change.

The balance has now shifted to the centre, and political control has led to a National Curriculum which is far too complex and prescriptive. Ministers have used their considerable powers to change it according to personal whim. The whole process has been watched with great dismay by people from other countries whose National Curriculum is usually contained in a single pamphlet. The two essential requirements are *a manageable single document* and *a degree of stability*, rather than alterations at monthly intervals. These plus the *ending of political interference* are vital for the health of a National Curriculum, which must be dynamic and changing, but on nothing like the scale we have had recently.

In the vision of life in the 21st century we described earlier, young adults will need considerable knowledge, a high degree of understanding, a range of skills, positive attitudes to what they are learning, in school and in the future, the flexibility and motivation to learn right through to old age, and the imagination and drive to lead fulfilling lives in work and in their family and social life. A curriculum based largely on the needs of assessment, which puts too high a premium on factual knowledge, gives too little emphasis to understanding and is tightly prescribed by the Government, cannot meet these aspirations. The process of lifelong learning should begin in the nursery school and then elide seamlessly into the infant school and beyond.

In infant schools a nine subject curriculum for five year olds makes no sense at all. Until children can read and write there is no point in making them study nine discrete academic subjects, plus RE. There should be a huge emphasis on *literacy* right at the centre of the infant school curriculum, from the very start. This should then be supported by four major domains: *numeracy, the arts* (including movement), *the world around us* (like *Heimatkunde* in Germany and Austria, knowledge of your own backyard, the village or the town in which you live), and *how the world works* (including science and technology). These *five domains* should not be prescribed in as much detail as the present nine subjects, yet they can embrace the best of what has been achieved so far. They should also permit plenty of practical and topic/project work, as well as quite specific targeted subject work where appropriate. Religious education remains part of the basic curriculum as it has been since 1944.

The early stages of junior school education should continue the five domains above, but with a shift in balance. Literacy remains central, but not quite as predominant as in the earlier stage, and the other domains, especially numeracy and the world and its workings, come into greater prominence. At age nine a move should be made towards more specific treatment of the separate subjects, with a greater degree of specialist teaching, though it should not be so heavily prescribed from the centre, maybe up to a third or 40 per cent of the week in the larger primary schools where this can be staffed.

Some National Curriculum subjects, like history, need thinning out considerably. There is no point at all in a rapid and superficial Cook's tour of the invaders and settlers, plough designers, pyramid and Parthenon builders, Tudors and Stuarts, Victorians and Aztecs. Better to understand fewer topics than dabble in too many. The same applies to the current Key Stage 2 technology, which is a conceptual mess, embracing as it does business studies, home economics and all the craft skills. More concentration on designing and making, cookery as cookery, not designing commercial food, and business studies as an awareness issue (under 'the world around us'), would make more sense. The whole lot should be pruned down to something that has a degree of breadth, but much more depth.

The early years of secondary need to be more of a bridge between primary and secondary than they are at present. There is nothing wrong with having ten subjects to study, but if we are serious about our membership of the European and international community, then consideration should be given to introducing a modern language at age nine, and having about four core subjects - English, maths, science, a modern language - and four domains - the arts, the humanities, technology, and physical and health education - as the basis of a curriculum from age nine up to fourteen.

Specialist topics in history and geography, for example, are perfectly feasible within a humanities framework, but some work in this field should be inter-disciplinary. Similarly it is important to have separate art and music lessons in the arts curriculum, but arts festivals and familiarity with the whole range of arts, including drama and dance, are essential to this age group. The early secondary years must be made conceptually manageable, or it will remain a complete nightmare for all concerned, especially if teachers have to assess every attainment target in every subject. Formal assessment could be confined to core areas only and teacher assessment could cover the rest.

From the ages of fourteen to eighteen education needs to be seen much more than is the case at present as a coherent process for all pupils, whether they are leaving school at the earliest opportunity or staying on for further and higher education. It is very important at the 14-16 stage for pupils to have choices. The inescapable core for the majority should be *seven* fields: English, maths, science, a modern language, a humanities subject, a practical subject chosen from arts and technology, and physical and health education. Those that want to do more should be able to opt for more, including a full second foreign language course. A short form of modern language curriculum should be available for those wanting to take a second language principally for conversational and communication purposes.

For the 16-18 group virtually everyone, except the Government, wants to see a broadening of studies, a better system of vocational education and much less division between the academic and vocational. The Royal Society is amongst those supporting a five A-level slate, so it can hardly be said to be an attack on standards to contemplate change, especially as entries for A levels in maths and physical sciences have declined alarmingly by the year, dangerouly reducing the proportion of the age group with higher qualifications in these vital subjects. Whether students embark on what are usually called the 'vocational' or the 'academic' track, they should be able to acquire both 'pure' and 'applied' knowledge, understanding and skills, and there should be parity of esteem for what they achieve.

FURTHER AND HIGHER EDUCATION

The future welfare of the country depends upon investment in people. In particular, that requires a transformation of the system of education and training which young people enter into at 16, the end of compulsory schooling.

We propose:

•   That all young people should remain in some form of education and training up to the age of 18;
•   That a much higher proportion of the age group should continue into higher education;
•   That the extension of further and higher education to many more young people (with different talents and aspirations) requires a thorough reappraisal of courses, and of the routes through them;
•   That conditions for ensuring quality of learning should be established;
•   That research of high quality should be maintained.

But we have argued that the system of market forces - of autonomous and competing institutions - is not the best way to achieve these goals. Good institutions suffer for the wrong reasons. Strategic planning is neglected, fundamental questions about aims do not get addressed, and ultimately quality is diminished.

During the last few years there has been a rapid increase in the number of young people who remain in some form of full-time education after the age of sixteen, with over 70 per cent staying on to at least seventeen and between a fifth and a quarter (compared with one in seven during the 1970s and 1980s) going on to higher education. This is a considerable achievement, although no doubt much of it results from the economic recession.

There have been, especially at the age of sixteen, developments in the courses and qualifications offered to this increased number.

*   National Vocational Qualifications (NVQ) are available, or are being developed, at five different levels (from very basic low level skills to professional competences) to cover all occupational areas. They are work based assessments, bring greater order into the world of vocational qualifications;
*   General National Vocational Qualifications (GNVQ) are being developed, parallel with NVQs, for young people who prefer a general education with a vocational bias, which should lead into higher education; recently level 3 or Advanced level GNVQs have been labelled 'vocational A-levels' by the Secretary of State;
*   A and AS Level qualifications have been 'tightened up' to meet criteria approved by the Secretary of State.

Thus, there is emerging a tripartite and socially divisive system of post 16 education, developed for different sections of the community, despite John Major's stated intention of ending the artificial divided between academic and vocational courses.

There has been a rapid change in the institutional framework for these courses which we have already mentioned:

*   Colleges of Further Education and Sixth Form Colleges have been incorporated - freed from the control of Local Education Authorities

*   The distinction between public sector and private sector higher education has been abolished, and there are now nearly 100 universities and a handful of colleges of higher education

•   The distinction between further education and higher
        education is increasingly blurred as universities franchise
        degree level teaching to the colleges

To fund these 'independent' colleges and universities, major
funding councils have been established - the Higher Education
Funding Council (HEFC) and the Further Education Funding
Council (FEFC). These distribute money according to formulae
which increasingly take account of 'productivity' and of
performance indicators such as measures of quality of teaching
and (in higher education) of research. At the same time, some
funding for vocational courses in further education has been
funnelled through the Training and Enterprise Council (TEC),
reflecting a consumer-led rather than provider-led mode of
funding.

There has been a shift in the funding of higher education
towards a disaggregation of teaching and research, with the
consequence that there is emerging a system of higher education
institutions, hierarchically differentiated according to funding and
to quality of research. At the same time that hierarchy less and
less reflects the different   'missions' which polytechnics,
universities and colleges of higher education once served.

These changes have brought about three kinds of problem:

•   **Fragmentation**
        The market created by the incorporation of colleges has
        meant that institutions compete rather than co-operate
        with each other and that school sixth forms, funded
        differently, are put at odds with colleges of further
        education with which they have so frequently worked
        together. The lack of LEA control has removed the one
        element that might facilitate strategic planning of scarce
        human and material resources at the local and regional
        levels. Courses are now run to meet the specific

customised meeds of local employers, a rather narrow horizon.

- **Lack of clear purpose**
  The 'mission drift', as polytechnics become universities and as further education colleges take on the cheaper end of the degree 'market', reflects a lack of clear institutional purpose linked to the needs of the increased number of students. There is a need for much closer matching of what students require (often very different from traditional sixth formers or university undergraduates) to teaching provision.

- **Tripartitism**
  The Government has stubbornly refused to reform an A Level system which narrows the learning experience of the most able, which fails a disproportionate number and which does not address the question of economic relevance. Furthermore, a system is being created which, far from opening up access to many, is funnelling students along particular differentiated pathways (the academic and the vocational) without the facility of moving from one pathway to another. Important questions of status are not seriously addressed. The damaging academic/vocational divide is maintained.

We have already stressed the importance of young people having a coherent education between the ages of fourteen and eighteen. In order to provide this, several principles must be asserted or reasserted:

- Further education and training is important for *all* young people up to 18, and should therefore be so organised as to be responsive to their developing interests and economic needs - not confined to particular pathways which are chosen by them (or for them), often on inadequate evidence, often at a very early age.

- There should be a unified system of courses post 16, leading to a single qualification, within which there can be different emphases - technical, aesthetic, mathematical, practical, etc. This would be achieved through a thorough going modular system in which considerable choice might be achieved between the so called academic and vocational elements. A system of guidance and counselling would play an essential part in supporting the student's search for a meaningful and satisfying pattern of courses.

- The new system of post 16 education should be based upon strategic planning of resources within a region, rather than upon short term market forces. The modular structure of courses would require co-operative arrangements between institutions.

- There should be continuity of education from 14 to 18, reflected in a continuous curriculum continuity and in a common system of continual assessment - so that any assessment of progress made at the age of 16 is not 'terminal'.

- There should be an obligation on employers to ensure that all young employees up to 18 are treated as trainees and are given proper training programmes linked to further education and leading to recognised qualifications. Moreover, those qualifications should be respected in the grants or wages paid - the value of further education and training must be perceived by young people in this very concrete way.

- The importance of the youth service at a time of growing alienation of some young people should be vigorously reasserted and it should be linked more closely in its distinctively educational role with schools, colleges and higher education.

- The system of higher education should have clear and national statements of strategic purpose, setting out different aims for different institutions to meet the requirements of both the economy the individual and the public at large.

- There must be financial support for all who participate in education and training post 16 and who otherwise would not be able to benefit from the provision.

- There should be national standards councils both for further education and for higher education, the aims of which would be to define more closely standards of performance, to ensure that colleges and universities have established systems of quality assurance, and to monitor the extent to which those standards are maintained. The membership of such councils should represent the teaching staff within further and higher education as well as other interested bodies, such as employers and the local community.

- There must be opportunities for continued education and access to education throughout life. This is essential not simply for personal satisfaction but also for ensuring the possibility of further education and retraining in a population which must constantly adapt to new economic and social contexts. Higher education institutions in particular must provide the modular programmes and the facilities which make for easy access and exit of mature learners, many of whom have other responsibilities than full-time learning.

- There must be a reduction of regulations, leading to a more significant place for the professional judgement of those engaged in education and training, albeit within a framework of strategic planning and of quality assurance. The autonomy of universities as centres of research, teaching and criticism must be preserved.

- At a time when the rising costs of expanding higher education could easily lead to the privatisation of universities and to dependence on private fees, there must be a system of personal support and of funding which ensures that no one is prevented from attending even the most prestigious university on financial grounds.

There is a revolution in post 16 education and training as more seek access to it. That raises important questions about curriculum, assessment, styles of learning, institutional framework, access and funding which are not being adequately addressed. The problem arises partly through the domination of the 'market' as the mechanism through which a coherent national system is to be created, and partly because of the maintenance of the academic/vocational divide in the courses, curriculum and assessment.

It is vital that further and higher education, which prepare young people for life and work in the 21st century, should be available to all, irrespective of background or wealth, should lay firm foundations, but also whet the appetite for lifelong learning, whether for its own sake, or for specific purposes like retraining. We shall return to the question of post-16 qualifications for all in the following section on youth, adult, community and continuing education.

YOUTH, ADULT, CONTINUING AND COMMUNITY EDUCATION

The Government's approach to youth, adult and continuing education and training has been an extension of its general approach to education - selection of the few for highly resourced academic education, and under-resourced provision for the rest. The exemplary youth, adult and community education services, with which Britain led the world, are now seen as of peripheral importance. Government appointed TECs are given what is seen to be the important training work, and LEAs are left to pick up what is left. Under a financial climate of diminishing resources for local services, youth, adult and continuing education have been the first to feel the brunt of cuts.

Faced with a barrage of reforms and financial cuts, those working in educational institutions or in LEAs have still continued to innovate and to improve provision and practice, building on achievements that are recognised and imitated throughout the world. Open learning methods, pioneered through the Open University, modular courses and qualifications to provide flexible modes of full-time and part-time study, access programmes giving disadvantaged adults opportunities to enter further and higher education, are just three examples where alternative education policies to those of the Government have been at the forefront of constructive educational change. All are under ever increasing financial pressure and need to be defended at all costs if continuing education is to be any more than a pipedream. Yet in our vision of the 21st century there should be educational opportunities for all, whether young people who have just left school, or those increasing thousands of people entering the Third Age of healthy retirement.

The seeds of a deeply divided system of separate academic and vocational tracks, curricula, institutions and qualifications are sown as soon as pupils reach adolescence. Examinations at 16

produce two groups of young people who move down two
clearly separated pathways. England is the only developed,
industrial country to insist on such early selection, which results
in weeding out so many pupils that only an elite is left to
continue into further or higher education. We need to move from
what Finegold has called an *early selection-low participation
system* to a *late selection-high participation system*, 'adequate to
the economic and social demands of the next century'.

In the more closely integrated 14-18 track we have proposed, the
strengths of A Levels and good vocational courses would be
preserved and enhanced with all young people experiencing
vocational as well as general and academic education. Many
National Vocational Qualifications are too narrowly job specific
and therefore not in the long term interests of either the
candidates or the nation. A modular system of general and
practical courses, offered in full-time and part-time mode and
using a variety of curriculum approaches, including open
learning and work-based experience, would not only lay a firm
foundation for further and higher education, but would also
create the bedrock on which lifelong learning could be based.
Modules of the kind normally taken by 14-18 year olds should
be available to *all* adults at whatever age they wished to start or
continue post-school education. It should never be too late to
learn.

We have already discussed changes that are necessary for people
in further and higher education in the previous section, and there
are four compelling reasons why radical change in the education
of all adults is needed:

•   We need to build on the welcome changes made at
        GCSE level where a more active style of learning has
        improved motivation and has raised the standard of
        achievement. A Levels still emphasise the passive
        absorption and regurgitation of factual information. The

A Level syllabuses (all 400 of them) are overloaded with factual knowledge. Adult learners are usually able to be fully involved in their own learning and are not empty vessels into which knowledge is poured.

• The whole system of premature specialisation means that English and Welsh pupils, alone in Europe, study ten subjects up to the age of 16, then two or three in the Sixth Form, and finally only one or two at University, closing down, rather than opening up possibilities. Many adults are excited by new opportunities to develop or unleash their talent.

• A Levels are predicated on failure; on average, about a third of those who take the exam do not receive a pass grade. Both the Audit Commission and the Office for Standards in Education (OFSTED) (1993) recently reported non-completion rates among 16-19 year olds of thirty per cent. It must be emphasised that these failures and drop-outs were, two years earlier at 16, the successes of the system who had passed GCSE exams; this represents a criminal wastage of human potential which we as a nation cannot afford. Failure at 16-18 often dulls or terminates the appetite for further learning. Many adults wrongly believe they are stupid, simply because school was a place of failure. Continuing education needs to emphasise 'success' and 'can do', not hark back to failure.

• If A Levels are retained in their present form, the National Education Target by the Year 2000 (of at least 50 per cent of each age group to attain NVQ Level 3 or its academic equivalent) will not be met. Opportunities for everyone, throughout life, to achieve the highest standards are essential. Reaching A Level, or its equivalent standard, at the age of 30, 40 or 70, would be a great joy for many older people who have missed out in their youth.

When money is short what suffers is the non-statutory elements of the service, like pre-school and continuing education. Youth, adult and community education should be restored to their rightful place as vitally important elements of educational provision, not left to the market and education cost-cutting. The attempt in Government policies to separate the academic from the vocational and the vocational from the recreational should be challenged by recognition that all forms of education are complementary and all serve a multitude of purposes. They should be brought together within a single continuing education framework in which personal and community needs are matched by appropriate and properly resourced educational provision. The separation of responsibilities between TECs for training and LEAs for education serves no useful purpose. Properly accountable Education and Training Authorities should be responsible for the whole of post 16 education and training. Critical to their acceptance will be representation on them on continental lines of *all* the social partners: politicians, employers and unions.

Equally all adults should have the opportunity to study and practise for its own sake, not just for vocational purposes - a language, the arts, a new hobby, a sport, writing, science and technology, information technology, cookery, or whatever. Education means freedom at any age, whether related to specific vocations or simply to fulfilling oneself and opening up the world of knowledge and skills.

The key to success in a situation of increasingly complex choices (beginning in the third year of secondary school and extending through to the late twenties) is advice and counselling tailored both to individual needs and to the labour markets. Education Authorities pioneered such ideas as Education Shops and Open

College networks. These will need to be rebuilt and integrated with the careers advisory services into a single system of advice and counselling.

The greatest problems for adults in completing courses are pressure from their domestic and family responsibilities, and financial difficulties. There are three ways of increasing the chances of success: modularity and flexibility in programme construction and delivery to enable students to complete courses to their own timetable; support services within institutions such as crèches; and financial support across the whole range of educational provision for those students needing it.

All educational institutions which so wish should be encouraged to serve the whole community. Many already open after normal hours to house youth clubs, adult education classes, leisure and recreation activities, but the provision is varied, excellent in some parts of the country, poor in others. There are several superb examples of community schools that are open seven days a week throughout the year serving everyone of whatever age and background who wants to learn. This model should become universal throughout the land, so that expensive educational plant and resources in town and country are available to all, cradle to grave, rich or poor.

SPECIAL EDUCATIONAL NEEDS

The history of special educational needs has been largely one of the exclusion of more and more children from mainstream education. Despite a rhetoric of 'integration' during the 1980s, and the inclusion of some children with physical or sensory disabilities who would formerly have been segregated, the number of children excluded from ordinary education in a variety of ways, continues to rise. This is a serious social as well as educational issue because modern societies increasingly demand qualifications and credentials acquired via a 'normal' education. To be excluded from mainstream education is to be excluded from the prospects of the employment and thus the mainstream of life.

Employers seldom look kindly on leavers from 'special' programmes. The majority of children who acquire any sort of a 'special' label are usually destined for a special career. Although special education is presented as ministering to the private difficulties of individual children, it is in fact a public issue, since it is designed to cater for the needs of ordinary schools to function unimpeded by children who are 'troublesome' (in the widest possible sense) and the needs of the wider society to recognise potentially burdensome citizens. Until recently the profit motive in industrial society directed that as many members as possible be productive. The question then arose as to how much of society's resources should be allocated to those who could not work..

After a hundred years of catering for what is now described as 'special educational need' the major arguments still focus on how to define those with special needs (the assessment process) and on the resources to be allocated to them. Assessment and resourcing have not been helped by the fact that there has never been a *national policy* to deal with special educational needs. Local authorities have been left to define special needs and make provision. An area where central government should have intervened more closely to provide national guidelines, continues to be a local responsibility.

Despite the rhetoric of integration, mainstream schools have always had strong reservations about accepting children who pose problems to their management, organisation, teaching and curriculum. Over the years, children have been referred for assessment as 'defective', 'disabled', 'handicapped', or 'having special educational needs', and, more recently, by segregation in behavioural units and straightforward exclusion. It has to be recognised that education establishment that develop mechanisms for removing the 'troublesome' have benefitted considerably. Teachers can concentrate on the education of the more able and the conforming, unimpeded by the undoubted problems which arise when difficult or disabled children remain in ordinary classrooms.

Over the past ten years, there has been an increased public and professional interest in, and dissatisfaction with, special educational needs (SEN). The 1981 Education Act linked the provision of resources to a 'statement' of a child's special educational needs, and extended the concept of SEN to include up to 20% of children. It created a demand from teachers and parents which LEAs were unable to meet and the Government did not resource. The emphasis placed by the 1988 Education Act on raising standards via a National Curriculum and testing, the publication of test scores in league table form, and the requirement for schools to market themselves to compete for pupils, have all conspired to make it unattractive for schools to take children with learning or behavioural difficulties.

As market competition has developed between schools, it has become obvious that some schools are competing for the more 'desirable' children and seeking to exclude others. Taken together, the two Acts have created a dilemma for the

Government. It is cheaper to educate children with special educational needs in mainstream schools (as required by the 1981 Act) but the operation of the 1988 Act makes such children burdensome. A further dilemma for the Government is that, having raised expectations that any identified special need will be provided for and that 'choice' of school will be available, new pressure groups are now pressing for provision (for 'dyslexia' for example) and demanding choice of school.

The narrow focus on assessment and 'choice' in *Choice and Diversity* reflects the present Government's concern to placate parents, but leaves the responsibility for assessment and statementing with the LEA - with no increase in resources. The White Paper also gives the unelected Funding Agency the power to turn Special Schools into Grant Maintained Schools.

The 1988 Act has created insoluble dilemmas in the area of special educational needs which will only be solved by changed policies. The *market economy* in which schools compete for pupils has made schools more conscious of their image, and predictably there has been an increase in the number of pupils excluded on grounds of behaviour and a rise in demand for statements of special educational needs. As schools become more image conscious, willingness to cater for SEN decreases, except where schools market themselves as dealing with special needs, or are willing to take the occasional 'able' statemented child with disabilities. Parents are expected to choose schools largely on academic achievement (via league tables), but this is usually not a consideration for parents of the 'specials'.

Other aspects of the 1988 Act are also contentious. Under local management (LMS) in mainstream schools, the annual budget contains an element for special educational needs, under formulae which are different in different LEAs. Heads and governors, however, can use the SEN element for other school purposes. The National Curriculum was originally intended to be an entitlement curriculum for all children, but measures for disapplying SEN pupils were built into the 1988 Act and others have been progressively introduced. The testing of pupils at key stages appears to be confirming those with special educational needs and the 'less able' in their status from the age of seven. Teachers fear for the child with learning problems permanently locked into Level 1.

Definitions of special educational needs have continued to be problematic since the concept was introduced by the Warnock Committee in 1978. Children put forward for assessment in one LEA (or one school) would not be put forward in others. Currently the concept embraces children with physical and sensory disabilities and children with severe learning difficulties, who as a group constitute less than 1% of the SEN and mostly have statements. The majority of those currently put forward for assessment and identified by mainstream schools as 'having SEN' have learning and behavioural problems in varying degrees. Keith Joseph in 1982 articulated a concern for the lower-achieving 'bottom 40%', and a Scottish report in 1978 suggested that 50% of pupils might have learning problems. There has also been a move to include the 'gifted' as having special educational needs. Schools can thus select between 1% and over 50% of children to target.

- In any alternative consideration of special educational need, we need to bring together discussion of special educational needs, school failures, under or low achievers, disruptive and excluded pupils.

- We would also wish to make clearer that the majority of the children falling into the above categories experience problems whose genesis may lie more in poor school management, and inflexible curriculum and inappropriate testing, poor teaching or poor teacher-pupil interaction than any deficit in the children themselves.

- Solutions to the problems must be found in school improvements, effective teaching, and teacher support rather than in more assessment, statementing or exclusion of children.

- Given the problems of definition and lack of clarity of the concept we should abandon the label of special educational need and envisage a broader concept which would embrace all children who find their encounters with the education system problematic.

- We wish to establish the principle that *all* schools, colleges and educational agencies are *inclusive institutions* which do not seek to exclude pupils on grounds of disability, inability, difficult or different behaviour. We want to defend this principle on grounds of social and distributive justice, of educational efficiency (pupils with SEN do better in mainstream) and of economic rationality (it is cheaper to educate all in mainstream schools).

- We want all schools, colleges and educational agencies to have high levels of staffing, resourcing and appropriate physical arrangements to deal with children and young people who are disadvantaged or experience difficulties in a particular school environment.

- We wish all staff to be professionally developed to high levels to accept that *all kinds of children will enter their classes to be educated* and that the management will develop policies and allocate resources to help teachers.

- We thus wish to move beyond arguments of integration versus segregation. In our view *all children* have a right to education in mainstream schools. We recognise, however, that a small number of those with severe disabilities who, with full parental consent, would need education outside mainstream classes. But even these could be given a place on the books of a mainstream school, should it ever be possible to attend it.

- We wish to end all secrecy and confidentiality that currently surrounds much of special education. (Some medical information may need to remain confidential.)

- We wish to end the legal coercion of parents whereby those who do not ultimately agree that their child will be placed in special provision can, under the 1981 Act, be fined or imprisoned.

THE TEACHING PROFESSION

Teaching is a profession because it requires:

- a body of knowledge to be learned
- a special set of professional skills
- an altruistic care for the client
- a collective responsibility for developing knowledge and practice
- a direct relationship of accountability for quality to both client and public

The last characteristic is the one that has become most salient recently, as the effects of a century of public education have created a more knowledgeable, demanding and participant democracy.

Yet teaching has not been accorded professional status in the public mind. There has been a long, slow progress towards an all-graduate and professionally trained teaching force. But in the public mind, teachers have been placed in the 'unproved and not-quite-accepted' group of semi-professionals. Moreover, to require all children to go to school means that adults have all had experience of teaching, so the best and the worst is remembered. Examples of professional *mispractice* in other fields seem to have less effect; teachers remain uniquely exposed.

It is essential to the well being and development of society that the special contribution made by teachers is valued and acknowledged. The yearning among parents and the public is for an education service of high quality. Governments can only do so much. Whether the government chooses loose or close control of the framework of education, it will always be the teachers who actually create the quality. That is done through every daily transaction with children and their parents. It springs from the personal commitment, knowledge and skill of each teacher.

Some of the essentials of professionalism are now threatened by the control the Government has seized of the curriculum and also, through assessment, of the methods of teaching. Taken only a step or so further this will make the school teacher into a mere functionary, an instructor, who has no responsibility for thinking independently and devising content and method from principle according to the nature and needs of the pupils. This notion has been reinforced by successive ministers' public criticism of teachers.

Since, in our vision of the 21st century, children will need to be able to think for themselves, go on learning for a lifetime, be able to solve now unimagined problems by applying first principles, and be able to do most of this in co-operation and harmony with others, building and changing teams as circumstances change, it is only logical that teachers themselves need to be encouraged to do all these things, rather than merely implement someone else's curriculum in an uncritical way.

The introduction by central Government of national controls or market forces cannot ensure quality in education. Only teachers can do that. The time has come to give the teaching profession a large measure of responsibility for its own regulation and development. To recognise that, and to enthrone it alongside the national curriculum, would be to create an education system that had a fighting chance of matching up to the awesome challenges of the next generation.

We believe that a national framework for the continuing professional development of teachers is essential to the pursuit of excellence in teaching, to the improvement of educational standards and to enabling the education service to respond to changing national priorities. This framework should integrate initial teacher education, professional induction and continuing professional development.

Some form of General Teaching Council functioning as a professional body for teachers in England and Wales could play a significant part in the development of the teaching profession, and we are at a loss to understand why Scottish teachers should have the benefit of a General Teaching Council, while teachers in England and Wales are denied the benefit of such an organisation. The time has come to establish similar agencies, entitlements and frameworks for the teaching profession as exist, through the General Medical Council, for doctors.

The requirements for implementing the 1988 Act have resulted in a concentration on short-term policy-specific and curriculum-specific issues. This has led to the abandonment of longer courses and a surfeit of single day courses. There should be a comprehensive programme for teachers at school, local and national level, with short day release and one term or one year secondments available, as suitable and feasible. National scholarships to support teachers' full- or part-time study would be a wise investment, removing the burden of finding the cash from schools and from individual teachers who increasingly have to finance themselves.

We are particularly concerned at the Government's policy on the initial training of teachers. Radical changes in the preparation of new teachers might be justified by acute staff shortages or if the professional judgement was that existing provision is seriously impractical or otherwise inappropriate. Neither is the case. Graduate unemployment is a current problem, and the 1992 HMI survey of new teachers indicates a high level of satisfaction in schools with the quality of their recruits. In fact, government policy is being driven by prejudice rather than by evidence or argument. Teaching children in the first years of schooling is seen as especially simple (or in John Patten's word, 'straightforward'), so that teachers for that stage need less general education and less training. 'Theories' of how children learn, and might learn more effectively, merely complicate the task unnecessarily and are in any case dangerously progressive and egalitarian. The initial professional preparation of teachers can therefore be entirely school-based without loss, the supply of training can be deregulated without risk, and such radical changes can be implemented without any substantial consultation with the profession itself.

Our alternative policy rejects those assumptions, and starts from the propositions with which this paper began. The insistence that all teachers should be graduates with additional, substantial and specialised training is not (as has been argued from the Right) the protective self-interest of a craft, but a proper recognition that teachers' work, always demanding, has become even harder as more is expected from schools and as the world of the 21st century for which children are being prepared seems likely to be ever more complicated. The co-equal partnership in that preparation between higher education and schools is not between theory and practice, with theory 'learned' in one context and 'applied' in another, because teaching is not like that. Much of the theory, in the sense of exploring and reflecting on professional practice, is inseparable from acquiring experience in the particular circumstances of a school and with the expert help of its teachers.

Many of the wider questions about school organisation and professional responsibility are also best confronted by beginning from, or focusing on, how particular schools (for example) seek a 'balanced' curriculum, support children with learning difficulties, allocate their budgets, interpret their accountability to parents, and monitor their own performance. The indispensable contribution of higher education to the partnership is to provide a wider frame of reference, encouragement to consider different ways of teaching well, and a commitment to introducing new teachers to research evidence and methods of inquiry relevant to developing their professional skills and understanding.

Most important of all is the commitment of higher education to constructively critical scrutiny of ideas and practices. As we have pointed out, the present Government has shown a marked tendency to take advice on education policy from a small group who share its prejudices. Though teachers, parents and school governors have shown willingness to resist authoritarian and ill thought-out directives, the independence of universities and colleges is a further, invaluable defence against the Government's preference for giving more and more power to publicly unaccountable bodies packed with its own nominees.

A substantial base in higher education is essential whatever the age of pupils which student teachers are preparing to teach. It is essential to avoid any unnecessary divisions in professional preparation which would impede professional unity and create categories of teacher differing significantly in status and conditions of work. It has been a particularly grievous error in Government thinking to assume that teaching young children is less intellectually demanding, so that teachers of that stage can be less well educated and more rapidly 'trained'. That assumption ignores both the extraordinary pace and range of learning before the age of seven and its fundamental effects on subsequent progress.

The partnership of schools and higher education has to be given time to develop through consultation, resourced at a level which recognises its importance to the future quality of schools, and properly monitored. Schools have to be adequately funded for the substantial commitment of staff time and expertise which is required from them, and on a basis which allows sensible long-term planning of how that commitment is to be met, without an unacceptable diversion from their primary task of teaching children.

Alternative routes into teaching already exist, differing in the nature and balance of school-based and higher education-based work, and such differences should be encouraged because there is no one best way. Whereas the present Government's approach to evaluating its own initiatives is to declare them a success on no evidence at all, almost before they have begun, the quality of new teachers is too important to be subjected to ideologically-motivated experiments. The outcomes of all forms of professional preparation must therefore be subject to the same criteria, which should refer not only to directly observable classroom competences but also to the professional knowledge and understanding in which they are grounded. Deregulating provision, as is threatened in the current experimental delegation to 'training schools', would be disastrous if it replaced qualifications having a national currency with individual school certification lightly validated, and if it sacrificed to some untested notion of practical relevance the complementary contributions of schools and higher education to preparing new entrants for this most demanding of professions.

CONCLUSION

We have produced this alternative vision of education for the 21st century because we reject the market-led, centrally controlled thrust of Government policy as embedded in its 1992 White Paper *Choice and Diversity* and much of its previous policies since 1988. We thoroughly condemn a strategy which sees children as commodities, parents as consumers, schools as competitive businesses, teachers as technicians, the curriculum as a set of bureaucratic requirements, accountability as narrowly conceived test scores put into crude league tables, further and higher education as factories, power as something to be held and wielded by ministers, local democracy as an institution to be crushed, and pre-school, adult and community education as a luxury for the few, rather than the right of all.

We do not propose here to repeat all the suggestions and recommendations that appear in the text. However, we have tried to develop a vision of the future that recognises the likelihood of lifelong learning, the need for a highly skilled, knowledgeable and well-informed citizenry in the 21st century, imaginative, flexible and willing to retrain in childhood, adulthood and through and beyond the Third Age of healthy retirement.

We have asserted values other than competition and the commercial view of education, values such as altruism, co-operation, fairness and an understanding of those with learning difficulties or from less than privileged backgrounds, hence our insistence on fair opportunities for all, not just a favoured minority. The tight bureaucratic control and packing of committees and decision-making bodies with Government nominees must cease, as must the suspicion and mistrust of teachers and others who work in the education service. Private and public forms of education should be put on a proper footing, without the one being endorsed at the expense of the other.

We want to see education as a well-found service, with proper buildings, equipment and teachers; a chance for all three and four year olds to have a nursery education; a curriculum that is not just manageable but challenging, that encourages teachers and pupils not straitjackets them; a coherent system of education for pupils aged fourteen to eighteen which recognises and nurtures all kinds of talents, not just those of the few; a wide range of opportunities for people after they leave school, open to all who wish to take advantage of them, without barriers to the poor, to those from the less privileged groups in society, people in work, or to the unemployed. We also want to see a strong teaching profession with its own General Teaching Council, properly educated, respected not constantly reprimanded by politicians and with opportunities for professional development and the upgrading of skills and knowledge.

We also want to see a positive partnership between the parents, teachers, governors who are involved in schools and colleges and the elected local and national politicians who are responsible for the overall running of the service. There should be real rights and entitlements for parents, not token ones, full support for governors, not just a handing over of responsibility without assistance.

Finally there should be a positive reaffirmation of the right of every child and adult to the very best education that can be provided, at whatever stage, from cradle to grave, irrespective of origin, wealth, social background, religion or ethnic group. It is a pity we even have to ask for it, for it should be a foundation stone and basic human right in every humane society. The market will not make a fair provision for the future. Only the wholehearted and passionate commitment of everyone to a different vision of education for all will achieve that.

Higher Education: Expansion and Reform
David Finegold *et al*
Oct 1992 ISBN 1 872452 58 2 £9.95

Higher education in Britain is expanding fast, but how can the pace of change be maintained? This report examines reforms of curricula, student funding, research and staffing necessary for a sucessful shift to mass higher education.

Partners in Change:
A New Structure for the Teaching Profession
Tim Brighouse & Michael Barber
July 1992 ISBN 1 872452 56 6 £4.95

Britain's teaching force is under strain. This report presents a radical new plan to bring professional 'associate teachers' into the classroom.

A British 'Baccalauréat':
Ending the Division Between Education and Training
David Finegold *et al*
July 1990 ISBN 1 872452 09 4 £10

Recommends a unified system of 16-19 education and training with a 'British Baccalauréat' at its summit. IPPR's pioneering proposals have been adopted by, amongst others, the Royal Society and the Labour Party.

'At last a distinguished body is bold enough to stand up and recommend radical reform.' *Sunday Correspondent*